For my sister, Renate

C. R.

"A Song About Myself" by John Keats from *The Complete Works of John Keats,* vol. 2, edited by H. Buxton Forman, Glasgow, Scotland: Gowars & Gray, 1901. Illustrations copyright © 2017 by Chris Raschka. All rights reserved. No part of this book may be reproduced, transmitted, or stored in an information retrieval system in any form or by any means, graphic, electronic, or mechanical, including photocopying, taping, and recording, without prior written permission from the publisher. First edition 2017.

Library of Congress Catalog Card Number pending. ISBN 978-0-7636-5090-2.

This book was typeset in Arapey. The illustrations were done in watercolor.

Candlewick Press, 99 Dover Street, Somerville, Massachusetts 02144. visit us at www.candlewick.com.

Printed in Shenzhen, Guangdong, China. 16 17 18 19 20 21 CCP 10 9 8 7 6 5 4 3 2 1

A Song About Myself

a poem by John Keats

illustrated by Chris Raschka

CANDLEWICK PRESS

There was a naughty Boy,

A naughty boy was he,

He would not stop at home,
He could not quiet be —

He took

In his Knapsack

A Book

Full of vowels

And a shirt

With some towels —

A slight cap
For night cap —
A hair brush,
Comb ditto,
New Stockings
For old ones
Would split O!

This Knapsack

Tight at's back

He rivetted close

And follow'd his Nose
To the North,
To the North,
And follow'd his nose
To the North.

There was a naughty boy

And a naughty boy was he,

For nothing would he do

But scribble poetry—

He took

An ink stand

In his hand

And a Pen

Big as ten

In the other,

And away

In a Pother

He ran

To the mountains
And fountains

And ghostes

And Postes

And witches

And ditches

And wrote
In his coat
When the weather
Was cool,

Fear of gout,

And without

When the weather

Was warm—

Och the charm

When we choose
To follow one's nose
To the north,
To the north,
To follow one's nose
To the north!

3.

There was a naughty boy
And a naughty boy was he,
He kept little fishes
In washing tubs three

In spite
Of the might
Of the Maid
Nor afraid
Of his Granny-good—
He often would
Hurly burly
Get up early
And go
By hook or crook
To the brook

And bring home
Miller's thumb,
Tittlebat
Not over fat,
Minnows small
As the stall
Of a glove,
Not above
The size
Of a nice
Little Baby's
Little fingers —

O he made

'Twas his trade

Of Fish a pretty Kettle

A Kettle —

A Kettle

Of Fish a pretty Kettle

A Kettle!

4.

There was a naughty Boy,

And a naughty Boy was he,

He ran away to Scotland

The people for to see —

Then he found
That the ground
Was as hard,
That a yard
Was as long,
That a song
Was as merry,
That a cherry

Was as red—

That lead

Was as weighty,

That fourscore

Was as eighty,

That a door

Was as wooden

As in England—

So he stood in his shoes
And he wonder'd,
He wonder'd,
He stood in his shoes

And he wonder'd.

Illustrator's Note

When John Keats was just twenty-two, he decided to get out of London and go for a walk. He had already begun and ended a career in medicine. He had published two books of poetry and was ready to tramp in the mountains with his friend Charles, as Wordsworth and Coleridge had done. He would live, and see, and think, and then let all this grow into the grand poetry that he knew was inside him.

Arrived in the hills of Scotland, he wrote a letter to his sister, Fanny. John Keats was the oldest of four children, three boys and a girl, and since the death of his mother, when even John was only fourteen, he was the head of the family. Their grandmother, who loved them dearly, appointed a guardian who, as it turned out, did not. He despised John's poetry and kept most of the money from their parents for himself.

Nevertheless, John followed his star, his art.

And at the end of traveling twenty miles through the mountains he wrote to Fanny: "We have walked through a beautiful country to Kirkcudbright—at which place I will write you a song about myself."

This is where his poem sits in the letter—a poem he did not think much of and which does not really have a title.

He died just three years later, in Rome, where he had gone to try to rid his lungs of tuberculosis, a sickness he may have contracted on his walk in Scotland.

John Keats is remembered as one of the greatest romantic artists of all time—an immortal—who wove nature, life, and love into a perfection of words; into poetry. He can also be remembered as a loving brother, who wanted to make his sister laugh with a funny little rhyme: a Song About Myself.

HUDSON R.
BROADWAY
COLUMBIA
125TH ST.
LENOX
HARLEM R.
BRUCKNER
BRONX KILL
RANDALL'S ISL.
CENTRAL PARK
110TH ST.
5TH AVE
FOOT BRIDGE
EAST R.
MILL ROCK
MANHATTAN ISL.
ROOSEVELT ISL.
RFK
WARDS ISL.
N
N. BROTHER ISL.
S. BROTHER ISL.
RIKERS ISL.
QUEENS
DITMARS
STEINWAY
ASTORIA
30TH ST.
BOWERY BAY
LaGuardia